W9-DHX-361

# EXTREME SPORTS BIOGRAPHIES™

# KEVIN JONES

## SNOWBOARDING SUPERSTAR

ANNA WEINSTEIN

rosen
central™

*For my son, Abraham*

Published in 2005 by The Rosen Publishing Group, Inc.
29 East 21st Street, New York, NY 10010

Unless otherwise attributed, all quotes in this book are a result of interviews conducted by the author.

**Library of Congress Cataloging-in-Publication Data**

Weinstein, Anna.
Kevin Jones, snowboarding superstar / by Anna Weinstein.
    p. cm. — (Extreme sports biographies)
Includes bibliographical references (p.   ) and index.
ISBN 1-4042-0068-1 (lib. bdg.)
1. Jones, Kevin, 1975 — Juvenile literature. 2. Snowboarders — United States — Biography — Juvenile literature. [1. Jones, Kevin, 1975– 2. Snowboarders.]
I. Title. II. Series.
GV857.S57W415 2004
796.939'092–dc22

                                2003023336

*Manufactured in the United States of America*

**On the cover:** Left: Kevin Jones at the 2001 Winter X Games, Big Air, Mt. Snow, Vermont. Right: Kevin Jones at the 2002 Action Sports and Music Awards, Universal City, California.

# CONTENTS

At four o'clock in the morning, most of us are tucked away in our beds, warm and cozy, without a thought of waking up. It will be hours before we hear that familiar sound of the alarm going off, reminding us that a new day is about to begin.

For a professional snowboarder, four o'clock in the morning marks the start of the day. While we're still slumbering away, Kevin Jones is hitting the snooze button, rolling over, and peering out his window to look at the sky. When he sees a clear sky and bright, shining stars, he knows he's going to have a day on the slopes.

Bracing himself for weather that might easily be -15° Fahrenheit (-26° Celsius), Kevin dresses in several layers of clothing. He drinks a pot of green tea and stocks a knapsack with a few energy bars, plenty of water, and, if he's lucky, a few slices of pizza left over from the night before. Outside, Kevin meets his cameraman and photographer. Together, shivering in the moonlight, they pack up their snowmobiles and head for the mountains.

Kevin Jones waves to the crowds before the 2002 Action Sports and Music Awards outside the Universal Amphitheatre in Universal City, California. While he enjoys being in the spotlight, his career as a snowboarding superstar is built on a solid foundation of hard work and dedication to perfecting his craft.

# CHAPTER ONE
## PROFILE OF A SNOWBOARDER

During the past several years, snowboarding has grown to be more and more popular as a winter sport. A mix of skiing, skateboarding, and surfing, its appeal is obvious: outdoor fun, mountain air, fresh snow, and exhilaration. Most ski resorts accommodate snowboarders, and on any given winter day you're bound to see more than just a handful of brave folks navigating the slopes with a snowboard.

A relatively recent invention, the sport of snowboarding had humble beginnings. In 1966, Sherman Poppen created the first snowboard for his daughter, who had been trying

Sherman Poppen created one of the first snowboards for his daughter in 1966. He called his invention the Snurfer. These precursors to today's snowboards are now collectors' items.

to stand up while riding her sled. Though snowboards didn't exactly catch on at the time, snowboarding has since grown into a lucrative industry, typically categorized as an extreme sport. Today, snowboarding attracts a variety of participants. Men, women, boys, and girls from countries around the world enjoy the sport.

To watch professional snowboarders at work, you might tune into the Winter Olympics or the X Games. At these competitions you will see many of the best snowboarders competing for the title, performing mind-boggling

Professional snowboarders often travel to remote locations to find challenging courses. Snowboarders Victoria Jealouse, Shannon Dunn, and Katrina Voutilainen (from left to right) took a helicopter ride to reach this slope in Utah.

tricks with seeming ease. But what is the difference between an amateur snowboarder and a professional snowboarder? What does it mean to be a professional snowboarder?

## The Professional Snowboarder

Not just anyone can become a professional snowboarder. In addition to mastering highly complex snowboarding skills or moves, a professional snowboarder is willing and able to handle a rigorous practice schedule, sometimes undesirable weather conditions, and long and exhausting days. When a professional snowboarder isn't on the slopes practicing, he or she could be filming for a movie, going on publicity tours and photo shoots, or even recovering from injuries.

A professional snowboarder definitely has an exciting life, but don't be mistaken: This is a tough and sometimes frightening job. Professional snowboarding moves are so exacting and difficult, the margin for error is extremely minimal. The daily risks are enormous, and many professional snowboarders suffer from serious injuries each year. In fact, it is the professional snowboarders, as opposed to the amateurs, who suffer from the most severe injuries.

However, according to Kevin Jones, the demanding routines and potential hazards associated with the sport are not enough to discourage a professional from continuing a snowboarding career. As Kevin says, "There's nothing quite like it out there."

## Who Is Kevin Jones?

With nine competitive X Games medals and a three-year-running title of *Snowboarder* magazine's Rider of the Year, Kevin Jones is one of the most decorated and respected snowboarders in the history of the sport. Though he typically competes only three times each year, Kevin's career is highly visible and he is a hero to many snowboarding fans, as well as to other professional snowboarders. He is known to have a fluid style and an uncanny ability to master the most difficult of tricks. He is the best of the best.

## Jeenyus Snowboards

In addition to being a champion snow-boarder, Kevin is also a successful businessman. His snowboarding gear company, Jeenyus Snowboards, was founded in 2001 and has proven to be a worthwhile business venture for Kevin. The company promotes the talents of up-and-coming snowboarders and many aspiring riders can be seen using Jeenyus gear.

This is the logo for Kevin Jones's company, Jeenyus Snowboards.

Kevin lives in the mountains of Bend, Oregon, where he has made his home since 2002. After spending ten years in the public eye, Kevin appreciates the anonymity he finds in Bend and relishes his time alone. He says, "When I'm in a snow town, I feel like I'm something. In Bend, it's cool because my friends are my friends because of me, not because I'm a snowboarding dude."

## Kevin's Family

Kevin was born in Sacramento, California, on January 23, 1975, and grew up in nearby El Dorado Hills. He describes his childhood as "picture perfect." His parents, Mitch and Peggy Jones, gave Kevin and his three siblings a solid upbringing. With regular church activities and a 9:00 PM curfew, Kevin's parents instilled in him a sense of honesty and integrity.

"My parents have been married for thirty-one years," Kevin says. "When I look back on my childhood now, I feel pretty fortunate to have been raised with my parents' values. I'm a lucky guy." Kevin remains close to his family. They talk and visit regularly, and Kevin is grateful for the time he is able to spend with them.

## Kevin's Childhood

When Kevin was young, he enjoyed reading, listening to music, playing music, and, of course, participating in sports. His favorite team sports were soccer, baseball, and basketball, but in seventh grade, he chose to give them all up in order to concentrate on skateboarding.

Kevin says, "One of my coaches told me that I couldn't skateboard anymore because there was a chance I could get hurt. That's when I decided to quit all the other sports and spend my time skateboarding."

Kevin found pleasure in the solidarity of skateboarding. and he came to realize that, in general, he preferred individual sports to team sports. Throughout junior high and high school, Kevin skated daily. At the time, skateboarding was not considered a "cool" sport, and Kevin and his friends were often picked on by other athletes at school. To avoid being ridiculed by his peers, Kevin would routinely hide his skateboard in his bag.

This may not seem like a great start to a career as a professional snowboarder, but as Kevin says, those same people who used to make fun of him in school are probably using his professional Jeenyus snowboarding gear today. Cool or not, Kevin's skateboarding practice paid off.

# CHAPTER TWO
# KEVIN AND THE SNOWBOARD

Kevin was seventeen when he first heard about snow-boarding, and he wasn't particularly impressed with the concept. In fact, he thought snowboarding sounded like a rip-off of skateboarding. He remembers, "I thought it was pretty stupid at first. I thought, 'What are these clowns trying to do, imitate skateboarding on the snow?'"

Kevin's skateboarding friends were also unimpressed with the idea. It wasn't until Kevin saw one of his all-time skateboarding heroes Noah Salasnek snowboarding on a video that he changed the way he felt about the sport. He

Kevin's first foray into snowboarding happened during a visit to the slopes in Squaw Valley, California. Here an aerial tram carries skiers to the top of the mountain.

figured if Noah Salasnek was doing it, he might as well give it a try.

A few days later, Kevin hit the slopes in Squaw Valley, California, and he hasn't stopped snowboarding since. He says, "After the first time, I just knew it was something I was going to do forever."

## The Early Days

Kevin visited Squaw Valley several more times and eventually became hooked on snowboarding for good. Soon after, he

moved to Truckee, California, for the sole purpose of snowboarding. Truckee was an ideal location for Kevin to perfect his craft; at an elevation of 7,700 feet (2,347 meters), the annual snowfall is 33 feet (10 m), and Truckee's longest mountain run is 5,280 feet (1,609 m). Already a highly skilled skateboarder at this point, Kevin picked up snowboarding quickly, mastering the complex moves with ease. Even so, Kevin was determined to be the best he could be—and that took practice. Kevin made it his mission to snowboard every day.

In the beginning, it wasn't always easy to come up with the money he needed to snowboard, so he had to find some creative ways to get on the slopes. Sometimes he'd get on a lift without a ticket, hike, or borrow a friend's pass. He recalls, "It just totally took over. I'd camp in my car in the parking lot if I had to, cheat—whatever it took." Though Kevin freely admits to employing these tactics, he doesn't recommend that his fans follow in his footsteps. He has respect and an appreciation for hard work and making money honestly.

Truckee is approximately an hour away from Kevin's hometown of El Dorado Hills, California. To raise money for snowboarding, Kevin was fortunate to be able to work

A snowboarder tackles the challenging terrain of Squaw Valley, California. After a few experiences on these mountains, Jones began a passionate pursuit to perfect his talents on the slopes.

## Snowboarding Hazards

It's important to remember that as glamorous and exciting as it looks, the sport of snowboarding is not without danger. Even the best of the best are susceptible to the hazards of the sport. Some professionals have actually lost their lives while snowboarding. For example, Craig Kelly died tragically in an avalanche in British Columbia, Canada. In fact, no extreme sports are risk-free—all the more reason to be as prepared as possible when jumping into a new sporting situation.

Pioneering snowboarder Craig Kelly, (1966–2003).

for his father's concrete company in El Dorado Hills. "My dad let me work whenever I wanted. So that was pretty cool. I'd drive back to my parents', wake up at six o'clock in the morning, and go to work for two days straight," Kevin recalls. After two days of work, Kevin would make enough money to snowboard for four or five days. He would make the drive back to his hometown every week, then return to Truckee ready to hit the slopes.

In the beginning, during the summers of 1993 and 1994, Kevin lived with his parents and worked for his father full time. After saving a sufficient amount of money,

Kevin moved temporarily to Mount Hood, Oregon, where he snowboarded for the remainder of the summer months.

Kevin remembers that though his parents were supportive of him, they were not extremely happy about him snowboarding all the time: "My parents didn't like it that I was spending so much time snowboarding because I couldn't make any money at it. I mean, now they're proud because we made something out of nothing. They're excited about it, which is good because you want to keep your parents proud, you know."

How could they not be proud? After just two years of snowboarding Kevin was picked up by a sponsor, Lamar Snowboards. Lamar paid Kevin to use the company gear while he snowboarded in regional and national competitions. What a deal!

And the rest is history. Since the early 1990s Kevin has become a snowboarding icon, and to many aspiring snowboarders, Kevin is seen as more than just a "Jeenyus" snowboarder—he is also a hero.

## Kevin's Heroes

When Kevin was just starting out, there were several snowboarders who influenced his style and his decision to pursue snowboarding. Kevin's snowboarding heroes, both then and now, are the late Jeff Anderson, whom Kevin describes as the "guru of railing," and the late Craig Kelly, in Kevin's words, "the godfather of freestyling." A handful of others have influenced Kevin's style, including Travis Parker, Marcus Egge, Josh Dirksen, Terje Haakonsen, Peter Line, J. P. Walker, Jussi Oksanen, and Jeremy Jones.

But Kevin's list of snowboarding heroes isn't limited to famous snowboarders. "I think anybody who gets out there, tries his or her best, and has a good time is a hero," he says. "There's nothing worse than a snowboarder who complains, because when you think about it, what's there to complain about? We're snowboarding!"

Kevin's skateboarding heroes are Jamie Thomas, Tony Hawk, and Noah Salasnek, to name a few. As a rule, Kevin has a deep respect for all athletes; he can relate to anyone who has a burning desire to do the best that they can do.

## Snowboarding Thrills

Kevin is always striving to do his best. He likes a challenge and the satisfaction that goes along with hard work and accomplishment. While Kevin is widely considered one of the best snowboarders in the world, he feels there's always room for improvement. His love and passion for snowboarding compel him to attempt the impossible, achieving and mastering what was before only a dream.

One of the things Kevin enjoys most about snowboarding is the feeling that he can do anything he wants to do. Because it is a sport that can be done in isolation, there are no teammates to depend on, and as Kevin says,

Jeremy Jones is one of many snowboarders who has influenced and inspired Kevin Jones. Shown here, Jeremy Jones navigates the daunting slopes of the Chugach Mountains in Alaska.

14620

"you don't need to worry about other people messing it up for you."

"I don't like being around lots of other people," Kevin admits. "I like hanging out alone or with just a few close friends and concentrating on what I like to do." For Kevin, this is snowboarding, plain and simple. Rather than performing for a crowd, Kevin feels at home with his friends, snowboarding for the sheer thrill of it. He appreciates snowboarding much more when he isn't being watched; this way he doesn't feel he's under a microscope, and he doesn't have to worry about being cool. He says, "When I'm not doing it for the money, it's almost like I see the snow as a blank canvas. Not to sound corny or anything, but I see all this beauty and I know I can do anything I want." Kevin explains that it's easy to become captivated by the wind and other noises in the wilderness.

Being a lover of nature, Kevin also enjoys the outdoor benefits of snowboarding, such as hiking and exploring the mountains. He says, "You're always in these really cool spots, and there's tons of stuff to check out while you're there." He likes to snowboard where there's fresh snow; depending on the weather and the year, Kevin has enjoyed the mountains of Canada, Alaska, and New Zealand. Though the mountains in Switzerland are a thrill and "totally awesome," Kevin finds them to be too massive to navigate on a regular basis. The fear of avalanches is real in Switzerland, and Kevin prefers to stick with the slopes ranging from 600 to 2,000 feet (183 to 610 m). In Kevin's words, "your chances of dying are much less on a smaller slope."

## Snowboarding Chills

In snowboarding, fear comes with the territory. Kevin confesses that he's scared almost every time he snowboards. In addition to avalanches putting snowboarders at risk, many snowboarding jumps are life threatening. Kevin has watched a number of friends end up with slipped or herniated disks or various other injuries as a direct result of participating in the sport.

Though Kevin and other acclaimed snowboarders make the sport look easy, those who have tried it can attest to its difficulty. Some of the most challenging moves require a precision that takes many hours of practice before mastering. A wild 1080-degree twist can lead to extreme injury if done incorrectly.

Kevin says, "When I take a month or two off, or when I get hurt, I start to wonder, 'Man what am I doing this for?' Late at night, I'm like, 'I want kids someday, I don't know if I want to be a part of this anymore.'" Of course, the next time he gets some air and perfects a cool move, Kevin remembers the appeal, and though the fear remains, the desire to succeed takes over.

# CHAPTER THREE
## THE SPORT OF SNOWBOARDING

The "Snurfer," the snowboard that Sherman Poppen created for his daughter in the mid-1960s, got a slow start in sporting-goods stores, but eventually more than a million boards were sold. Although it wasn't until the early 1990s that the sport really took off, Poppen's creation appears to be the beginning of the mass appeal of snowboarding.

Jake Burton is considered by many to be the pioneer of modern snowboarding. Burton rode his first Snurfer when he was fourteen and so began his interest in snowboarding. Eventually, Burton went on to design the first

Jake Burton *(left)* began snowboarding at the age of fourteen. His board collection includes the designs he created for his own company, Burton Snowboards, as well as the Snurfers that inspired his career.

snowboards that resemble the boards professional riders use today. Burton Snowboards is still one of the top snowboarding companies, and many professional riders use Burton gear.

However, over the years there has been some discussion as to the true origin of the sport. The roots of snowboarding can be traced back to the early 1920s. At that time, children in Vermont created their own "snowboards" out of barrel slats. And before that, soldiers in World War I are said to have slid down hillsides on handmade snowboards in Europe. Regardless of who can take credit for being the true inventor of the sport, the allure is clear: where there's a hill and snow, there's bound to be someone riding a snowboard. Just don't be fooled—this isn't as easy as it looks!

## Beginning Boarders

Kevin and his colleagues have an uncanny ability to make snowboarding look simple, but it's important to remember that perfection takes practice. Snowboarding can be a high-risk sport and it is essential to be prepared and knowledgeable before beginning for the first time. Here are some things an aspiring snowboarder should consider:

- Get in shape

- Learn about the different snowboarding styles

- Learn about the proper gear

- Learn the snowboarding moves slowly, one at a time

### Getting in Shape

Professional snowboarders make it their business to stay in shape. And that doesn't just mean working out. Snowboarders have to eat plenty of healthy foods and drink plenty of water. They also have to be sure to get lots of sleep. There's no such thing as staying up all night and then hitting the slopes the next day. Self-respecting athletes understand that they need all of their faculties in top-notch order to get their best performances. They take care of their bodies and build regular exercise, sleep, and nutrition into their routines.

In addition, professional boarders ride with extreme care. They do not casually attempt dangerous, difficult moves without first preparing for and building up to the skill. A smart rider knows when a particular move or snowboarding style is beyond the scope of his or her abilities. This self-knowledge is essential for snowboarders to protect themselves from injury.

## Snowboarding Styles

Over the years, various styles of snowboarding have been developed, or in some cases, the styles have simply been given a name. For instance, some snowboarders prefer to freeride, while others prefer to ride in the pipe. Prospective snowboarders should get a grasp on the styles of snowboarding so they can talk freely about the sport and make educated decisions before riding.

Freeriding, or freestyle, is the heart of snowboarding. This is the most basic type of ride: a rider on a mountain, doing whatever feels right, exhibiting his or her own personal style. The name indicates the freedom associated with the style—this is an anything goes kind of ride.

Backcountry riding is an exciting, thrilling, and potentially dangerous style of snowboarding. This is riding in the wilderness, where the terrain is steep and the challenges are much greater than they are at a ski resort. Backcountry riding is only for the most experienced snowboarders— and should always be done with a buddy.

Pipe riding originated with skateboarding. A half-pipe is a U-shaped snowboarding ramp. Snowboarders ride the pipe, crossing from one side to the other.

Bordercross is a ride in which up to six snowboarders race down a mountain. The first to cross the finish line wins. This is a genuine peer-judged ride—with no actual judges present. This style of snowboarding is typically reserved for very experienced riders.

Alpine boarding is for riders who enjoy high speeds and racing. Alpine boarders have been clocked at more than 90 miles (145 kilometers) per hour!

Snowboarders of all ages enjoy different styles of snowboarding, and many riders even have a preferred style.

## Snowboarding Gear

Whether freeriding or alpine boarding, it's essential that a snowboarder get in shape, sharpen his or her skills, and use the proper equipment and gear. The first thing a snowboarder needs is a board, boots, and bindings.

Boards come in varying lengths and widths to accommodate different body types and different styles of riding. Snowboarding boots should be comfortable and snug but shouldn't pinch or hurt the feet or ankles. Most snowboarders wear soft boots that provide warmth and

**Luke Mitrani grabs the heel side of his board as he sails above the Superpipe during the qualifying round at the January 2003 U.S. Snowboard Grand Prix competition in Breckenridge, Colorado.**

Bindings

Goggle

Boot

Helmet

In addition to buying the appropriate boots, bindings, and boards, the proper safety gear is extremely important. Experienced riders never hit the slopes without a helmet, goggles, and wrist guards.

flexibility. Bindings are like seat belts, fastening a rider's feet to the board.

Perhaps the most important gear of all is the safety gear. Professional and amateur snowboarders alike wear safety gear when riding at a resort or in the backcountry. Goggles protect the eyes from the snow and sun, wrist guards protect the wrists from a fall, and most important, a helmet protects the head. Ask any experienced riders and they're bound to tell you that safety gear is their best friend. No one should be caught boarding without it.

## Advice to Aspiring Snowboarders

To learn the basic and the more radical moves and tricks, many professional snowboarders advise beginning riders to work with an expert boarder or coach. There are lots of different moves and grabs and holds, all with cool names that can be somewhat overwhelming for a beginning rider. A sampling of the snowboarding moves includes ollies, nollies, and fakies. There are toeside, heelside, frontside, and backside turns, twists, or spins; method, indy, mute, or tail grabs; or the more complex seat belt, walt air, crail, and nuclear air grabs. The toughest grabs of all have names such as chicken salad air, flying squirrel, Swiss cheese air, and spaghetti air.

Kevin Jones has a few pieces of advice for beginner boarders. First and foremost, he says, "just enjoy it and have fun—everything else will come. And if it doesn't, at least you're having a good time. It's a win-win situation." Second, Kevin advises beginners not to worry about going pro or getting in snowboarding videos. "If you're good, they'll spot you," he says. "You don't have to do anything special or try to prove that you can do a certain trick. Just ride. If you're good enough, you'll be seen. And if not, just keep on snowboarding."

# CHAPTER FOUR
## WHAT'S IT LIKE TO BE KEVIN?

Kevin spends most of his time snowboarding. When he isn't injured or doing publicity to promote his company, Jeenyus Snowboards, Kevin is rising early in the morning and tackling the mountain snow for an intense workout. In his home in Bend, Oregon, Kevin has situated his bed next to his window so he can easily check the weather status. When his alarm goes off at 4:00 AM, Kevin looks out the window at the sky. If it's cloudy, he goes back to sleep. If he sees stars, he knows it will be a clear day and that it's time to get out of bed.

It takes an incredible amount of dedication to get to the level Kevin Jones has reached in his sport. Kevin often wakes up at 4 AM to get in a full day of practice.

Waking up at 4:00 AM can get pretty tiresome, especially when you're exercising six to eight hours a day. Why does Kevin have to get up so early? Whether he is snowboarding in Lake Tahoe or Alaska, Kevin is usually accompanied by a cinematographer and photographer, who document his moves for professional snowboarding videos. Since filming is light-oriented, it is essential that there is enough light while shooting, and it isn't productive to shoot in the gray. For that reason, Kevin and his crew have to get to the selected spot on the mountain before the sun comes up.

## Video Mania

Kevin spends much of the year filming snowboarding videos. The videos showcase his awesome talents and offer aspiring snowboarders an opportunity to learn from the best. Snowboarders around the world watch Kevin's videos and emulate the moves they see him perform. Some even attempt to get cast in the videos themselves!

A fan checks out Kevin Jones on the cover of the *411 Video Magazine* DVD.

On a clear day, Kevin consumes a pot of green tea and a quick breakfast, and then dresses in several layers of clothing to prepare for the cold. Outside, he loads up his snowmobile and meets his cinematographer and photographer. Together, they ride out to the mountain. Kevin says, "Sometimes you'll wake up in the morning, get all the way out there, and the clouds come in. Then you can't shoot."

At the spot they select, Kevin waits for the sun and then performs his "sick" (really excellent) jump. Meanwhile, the cinematographer and photographer document everything. After the jump, they quickly move to the next spot as the sun works its way around the mountain. "You have to be pretty strategic—knowing that you're going to do this thing first and this thing second. Hopefully you know the area, but most of the time you don't," Kevin explains.

Depending on where they're located, Kevin and his crew stay in a hotel, an RV (recreational vehicle), or sometimes, some sort of base camp. Generally, they all have their gear ready the night before. The cinematographer and photographer have their equipment prepared, and Kevin has his boards waxed and ready to go.

Kevin will typically snowboard until two o'clock or three o'clock in the afternoon. Around that time, the light begins to change, and photographing the jumps is no longer productive. Besides, by that time, Kevin has been snowboarding for almost eight hours, not to mention hiking the mountain in between jumps. Kevin will usually be home (or at the hotel) around 5:00 PM and sound asleep an hour later. He says, "Snowboarding is really strenuous on your body and I'm usually in a lot of pain by the time I'm done. I pretty much crash as soon as I get home."

To complete a really "gnarly" day, Kevin will go into town in the evening and go jibbing on handrails. If it is snowing, the photographer will bring the lights and generator and set up the shots, as Kevin says, "Rambo style." Since it is illegal in most towns to film without proper permission and paperwork, Kevin and his crew are often dodging the police to get the shots. "Sometimes you get busted, sometimes you don't," Kevin admits.

## Kevin's Clothing and Gear

Packing up the snowmobile in the morning is no easy feat. The snowmobile has many different compartments, and Kevin has a massive amount of gear to bring along for the ride. Besides food and water, Kevin has to pack clothing and safety equipment. To keep himself warm in the winter chill, Kevin usually brings extra socks, underwear, gloves, and a down jacket—and these are just the extras. Kevin explains, "Every time you tumble you get wet, so you need to bring extra clothes. Otherwise you'd freeze out there."

In the morning, the weather ranges from -15°F to 8°F (-26° to -13°C), and in the afternoon it ranges from 10°F to 45°F (-12°C to 7°C). To accommodate and prepare himself for the varying weather conditions, Kevin dresses in several layers of clothing. He typically wears polypropylene clothing for the first layer and expedition-weight polypropylene or wool for the second layer. He wears a shell, a pair of down pants, a down vest, and a down jacket, and to protect his face and neck from frostbite, he wears a balaclava. In addition, Kevin wears a hat, gloves, glasses, and goggles.

Also packed in the snowmobile is his safety equipment. Every day, Kevin packs a cellular phone, a peep (or transceiver), a probe, and a shovel, and he sometimes carries a satellite phone. These are essential safety items to have, especially when snowboarding in the backcountry. In the case of an avalanche or getting buried beneath the snow, peeps allow snowboarders to

Snowboarding expeditions require a lot of preparation. Before heading out, Kevin packs his snowmobile with plenty of food, water, and extra clothing and boards. Kevin never forgets his safety gear, which includes a cell phone and shovel (both pictured above), as well as a transceiver and probe.

indicate to their companions where they are buried. The companions use probes to locate a buried snowboarder.

Kevin takes at least two snowboards, or "sticks," on his expeditions. He uses six different Jeenyus boards, ranging in length from 147 to 167 centimeters. Depending on the conditions and the tricks, twists, or spins he's performing, Kevin employs different types of boards. For instance, he

uses the 167 in deep powder, the 157 in a snowboard park with no powder, and the 147 on handrails. Because Kevin prefers boarding in deep powder, he tends to use the 167 most often.

## Kevin's Diet

With Kevin's demanding workout, it's important that he take in a sufficient number of calories to sustain his energy level. Over the years, Kevin has tried many different diets; from vegetarian to high protein, Kevin has seen them all. He has taken supplements, drunk smoothies in the morning, eaten energy bars in the afternoon—all in an effort to find the most complete, balanced diet. But Kevin hasn't found any particular combination of food and supplements that works better than others. He has found that some diets definitely do not work for him. He recalls, "The worst diet I ever tried was vegetarian. I was just so tired all the time, man."

These days Kevin doesn't stick to much of a diet. In the morning, he will sometimes make a quick stop at a 7-11 to fuel up with a quick breakfast before the day begins. For lunch, he'll often eat energy bars, leftover pizza, apples, and sandwiches and drink plenty of water. In the evening, it's whatever he can find quickly and easily.

Kevin makes it look easy, but pulling moves like this one requires a lot of practice and skill. To maintain his energy level during practice runs and competitions Kevin eats a lot of food.

## Railing

On snowy evenings during the winter months, in many big ski resort towns, you're bound to find a snowboarder railing. Railing is literally snowboarding down a handrail or a set of outdoor steps. Though skilled snowboarders can make this look easy, many will tell you that railing is particularly difficult and potentially dangerous. This snowboarding technique is not for amateurs!

Kevin Jones approaches the rail during a competition at the 2002 Winter X Games in Aspen, Colorado.

He says, "I figure if you're burning it off during the day, it's not that big of a deal what you eat."

## Kevin's Exercise Routine

It's not hard to imagine Kevin burning the calories he consumes each day. A six- to eight-hour daily exercise routine is pretty significant, and it doesn't leave him much time for any other form of exercise. Besides snowboarding and the endless hiking that goes along with the sport, Kevin does a lot of stretching to keep his muscles limber. When he finds the time, he lifts weights, focusing primarily on the upper body. "Nothing I do ever helps me get any upper body strength, so I try to work out my back and arms whenever I can," Kevin says.

Some people may think that all professional athletes have personal trainers, but Kevin has such a terrific support system among his snowboarding friends he doesn't need a personal trainer. Since he spends so much of his time snowboarding with friends, he always has someone to encourage him and help him recognize how he could improve. Besides that, he says, "In snowboarding everybody's his own personal trainer."

Kevin spends a lot of his free time skateboarding. He tries to skateboard every day during the summer, filling in with other forms of exercise, such as wakeboarding, in-line skating, white-water rafting, and fly-fishing.

# CHAPTER FIVE
# KEVIN'S CAREER

Kevin doesn't look at snowboarding as a career. Though he gets up every morning and goes to work, he realizes that snowboarding isn't a conventional occupation. As he describes it, "It's a way of life." Way of life, career, profession, job, work—whatever you want to call it, Kevin has had enormous success snowboarding.

Kevin entered his first snowboarding competition soon after moving to Truckee. Encouraged by his friends, who were also thinking of entering, Kevin looked into it and found that for $50 he could get a lift ticket, food, an invitation to a

The snowboarding world recognized Kevin Jones's talents soon after he made the move to Truckee, California. Here, he struts his stuff at the 2002 Sims Invitational in Whistler, Canada.

party, and a T-shirt, and he could potentially win $100 worth of gear. As it turned out, it was money well spent. Kevin won his age group and went on to enter and win several other regional competitions that year. "It was fun," he says. "I made a little extra money and I knew everybody there, so I had a good time."

## Going Pro

During his first year in Truckee, Kevin went pro. Going pro in 1993 was very different than it is today. Kevin humbly excuses his sudden success, saying that it was easier to be a professional then because there weren't any guidelines as to what "professional" meant. He says, "Everybody knew everybody. It was like a really close-knit family. Word traveled fast, so if there was a good rider out there, everybody knew it right off the bat."

In Kevin's case, success was very sudden. One day, a Lamar Snowboards rep saw Kevin snowboarding and simply walked up to him and handed him a board. He asked him to try out the board and said he'd have someone give him a call on Monday. Kevin was shocked. He explains, "I'd been snowboarding at that point for probably about six months and I'm like, 'How does this guy think I'm any good?'"

Apparently the rep knew what he was looking for. Maybe it was the years of skateboarding practice, the six solid months of snowboarding, or just natural talent—regardless, Kevin's professional career was about to take off.

That Monday, Kevin received a phone call, and for the next seven years he was represented by Lamar Snowboards. Kevin helped promote Lamar Snowboards by showcasing the equipment during professional competitions, and Lamar gave Kevin a modest travel budget.

In 1993, Lamar Snowboards became the first company to offer Kevin Jones a sponsorship. Jones still promotes their products and uses them during competitions like this one at the 2002 Sims Invitational.

Though things were tight, he was bringing in enough money to pay his rent, and he was able to quit working for the concrete business. He remembers, "I wasn't saving any money and I couldn't afford to buy anything nice. I had a car, but I was just barely making the payments." Every couple of months Kevin got a small raise, and somehow, he was able to make it work. "I just kept snowboarding and snowboarding." he recalls. "It's kind of weird how it all comes together."

In 1997, Kevin was recruited as one of the first clients of the Familie, a management company for athletes. Aided by proper agency representation, Kevin's career began to reach new heights. He started getting some of the best parts in snowboarding videos, winning major competitions, and doing publicity photo shoots and tours. In 2002, Kevin was featured in an X Games commercial shot in Los Angeles.

At the height of his success, Kevin is humble about his snowboarding career, insisting that he still has room for improvement.

## Thoughts on Success

Kevin tries not to think about how successful he's become. He says, "I've seen so many people get weirded out about that kind of thing, you know. They start thinking they're better than everybody else, or they're too cool, or they just do weird stuff. I pretty much try to stop my brain from thinking about any of that stuff. I tend to shut those thoughts off pretty quick." Kevin realizes that success isn't just about skill and talent; he knows it's about hard work, persistence, and even

## X Games!

In 1993, ESPN put together a team of people to conceptualize a framework for exhibiting the talents of alternative sport athletes. The first X Games competition, originally called Extreme Games, was held in 1995. Because of the "extreme" success of the first event (198,000 spectators attended), ESPN decided to hold the event again the following year. Since then, the X Games have become a regular source of excitement for extreme sports fans and participants around the world. Snowboarding, skiing, and snowmobiling are just a few of the extreme sports featured at the X Games.

luck. He feels lucky to be able to snowboard professionally, and he refuses to think he's better than anyone else.

Don Bostick, who organizes the skateboarding and snowboarding events for the X Games, has known Kevin since the early days. He describes Kevin as sensible, saying, "Kevin is very grateful for the level of success that he's achieved. He realizes that it could change tomorrow, and he manages to make light of things and not take himself too seriously." Bostick explains that Kevin's success is largely due to his positive attitude and his desire to better himself. When Kevin first realized that he had something special, he spent hours and hours perfecting his riding skills. The bottom line: success didn't just happen for Kevin; Kevin made it happen.

A regular part of Kevin's routine is publicity, and he spends a good deal of time each year meeting and greeting his fans. He enjoys spending time with his fans, learning about their passions and goals, and even snowboarding with those whom Jeenyus Snowboards might be interested in representing. He says: "I never picture myself as an icon. There are lots of kids out there with tons of talent. It's pretty cool to meet them and see how stoked they get."

## Achievements

Of all of his successes, Kevin is most proud of two things: the Rider of the Year title and a trick he performed at the 2000 X Games. The Rider of the Year title is particularly important to Kevin because it's a peer-judged competition; the voters are all from inside the sport, snowboarders themselves. This is important to Kevin because he respects the snowboarding talent of the judges, so he can feel good about their decision.

During the 2000 X Games, Kevin performed the frontside 450, a trick that only one other person had ever done before (the late Jeff Anderson). Kevin didn't need to perform the trick in order to win the contest, but for some reason he felt compelled to show everybody that it could be done. "It was just a weird little moment," he remembers. "I didn't want to just win the contest. I wanted to do this trick. I just needed to do it. I don't know why. I made up my mind right before I went on my run, I was like, 'Well, I already won a couple of these and I want to do it, so . . .'" And the rest, as they say, is history.

## Failure

Kevin doesn't believe there's any such thing as failing when it comes to snowboarding. He's a firm believer that

Actress Darryl Hannah presents the Male Snowboarder of the Year Award to Kevin Jones at the ESPN Action Sports and Music Awards in April 2001.

everything happens for a reason, so even the mistakes and injuries don't count as failures in his book. He says, "I don't ever think I've failed dramatically. Maybe there are things I could do better, but I don't think that I've really failed."

He considers snowboarding to be a blessing, in his words "a good, positive thing." The downside for Kevin is getting older, getting hurt, or being away from family

## Kevin's Competitive History

Despite the fact that Kevin prefers to compete with himself, he has had quite an impressive competitive history. Since 1999, Kevin has taken first place in a number of highly publicized competitions. That year, he finished an impressive first in the Vegetate competition in big air and slopestyle disciplines in Mount Hood, Oregon. In 2000, Kevin took first place at the Gravity Games competition in the big air discipline in Mammoth Mountain, California, and he placed first in the Winter X Games, again in the slopestyle discipline. In 2001, Kevin placed first at the World Championships in the jib jam discipline in Whistler, Canada. That same year, he placed first in the slopestyle discipline in the Winter X Games. With such a remarkable competitive history, Kevin's fans have high hopes for his future competitions.

and friends. "That's the horrible part about it," Kevin says. "Sometimes I get really burned out on the road—that's a definite low point."

Twenty-eight is the beginning of retirement for some snowboarders, and Kevin admits that getting older is something that bothers him. He's already experiencing some of the signs of aging; his back isn't as flexible as it used to be and he finds himself knocked out now at the end of a hard day. Kevin has to keep all of this in mind when he's snowboarding, otherwise he'll be even more prone to injury.

## Injuries

Getting hurt is what Kevin is most afraid of. Though he's never had any serious injuries as a result of snowboarding, he's well aware that the potential is there. But for now, it's the injuries he's suffered while participating in other sports that have taken him out of commission for months at a time.

After hurting his ankle playing basketball in 2001, Kevin was out for close to eight months. He recalls, "Luckily I did it in June, so I was ready to snowboard again in February." Then, in the summer of 2002, Kevin broke his arm skateboarding in Oregon. The doctors repaired his arm, but he still had several months of physical therapy ahead of him.

# CHAPTER SIX
## SNOWBOARDING AND BEYOND

Although snowboarding was part of the 2002 Olympics in Salt Lake City, Utah, Kevin chose not to participate. It was a very practical decision. According to Kevin, when snowboarding was just starting out, many professional snowboarders frowned on competitions. He says that because the judges were not in the snowboarding industry and had little insight as to what makes one snowboarder better than another, a lot of professional snowboarders felt it wasn't worth their time, nor was it respectable to participate in the competitions. Kevin explains that things have been

Kevin Jones believes that snowboarding is about pushing yourself to achieve, not about competing with others.

• • • • • • • • • • • • • • • • • • • • • • • • • • • • • • • • • • • • • • • • • • • • • • •

changing in recent years and the competitions have been getting better as the money gets better. Nonetheless, Kevin is not very interested in winning competitions.

He says, "I don't think I'll ever do the Olympics. It's just not for me. To me, the heart and soul of the Olympics is competition, and that's just not what snowboarding is about." Kevin has a great deal of respect for Olympic athletes, but he feels that snowboarding is not a competitive sport. In fact, Kevin believes that one of the reasons snowboarding caught on so well was because it wasn't competitive. Kevin explains, "If I go out and ride with a kid one day and I'm doing a frontside 1080 and he's learning a frontside 180, we can have exactly the same fun together. I'm just as excited for him as he is for me. You're only competitive with yourself."

Kevin appreciates the fact that snowboarders tend to help one another. He says, "I don't care if a friend of mine does better than me that day, 'cause I'm just so happy for the guy for doing well. It's not a competitive deal at all—at least for me it's not." Whether that is true of all snowboarders, Kevin's attitude toward competition is seen as inspiring and refreshing throughout the snowboarding community. He is widely known as a supportive friend and fan of other snowboarders.

Tom Collins, executive director of the USA Snowboarding Association (USASA), describes Kevin as "the epitome of a sportsman." Collins says, "Snowboarding is an individual sport. At USASA events, we encourage the participants to compete against themselves—to try and be the best they can be." Collins explains that most professional snowboarders live by the "competing against yourself" motto, but Kevin, he says, is the leader of the movement. Collins says that many snowboarders look up to Kevin when it comes to keeping a good attitude, having fun, and making sure that other people are having fun as well.

Perhaps Kevin's positive attitude has played a role in his success. Between the rigorous workout schedule, the less-than-ideal weather conditions, and the dangerous elements, it might be surprising that Kevin can maintain his bright outlook. Motivation is a necessity in the sport of snowboarding, and Kevin has found that competition has no part in motivating him to be the best he can be.

## Motivation

Kevin's love for snowboarding keeps him motivated even on the most difficult days. Because the retirement age for snowboarders is relatively young, Kevin knows that his time on the slopes is limited. He says, "Ultimately I have to answer to myself. I have to think about what I want to accomplish in this short period of time that my body will let me accomplish it." Kevin has friends who had a lot of snowboarding goals, but their bodies have reached the point where they simply won't comply with their wishes. Kevin is determined to accomplish his goals before his body gives out.

How does Kevin know that snowboarding is what he's supposed to be doing with his life? He responds, "I don't know. There's just some weird little thing in my brain that tells me that's what I'm supposed to be doing. That's my so-called meaning of life."

But it's not all fun and games. Like any profession, snowboarding has its downside, and even snowboarding can become mundane after doing it for a long time. As Kevin says, "Anything you do . . . over and over again becomes something you're not necessarily going to look forward to." Kevin always enjoys himself once he's on the slopes or doing publicity, but thinking about waking up at four o'clock in the morning isn't always exciting, nor is spending extended periods of time away from his family and friends. He admits, "It can get frustrating with the early mornings and the cold weather. It can seem really hard sometimes."

Despite the hardships and frustrations, Kevin perseveres. It's the joy he feels while catching air off the side of a mountain, or the look of excitement on people's faces when they meet him for the first time, or the simple pleasure he gets from lying in bed at night and recounting a particularly thrilling and successful day. These are the things that keep Kevin coming back for more.

## Beyond Snowboarding

Like most people, Kevin has many interests and passions outside of his profession. He enjoys listening to music, anything from Beethoven to Merle Haggard, to Willie Nelson and Frank Zappa. When Kevin was in high school, he played bass guitar in two bands: a punk fusion band called Yukon Cornelious and a jazz band called the Kurt Hebtche Trio. Kevin still enjoys picking up the guitar from time to time and plucking out a tune.

Kevin also enjoys camping, traveling, exploring new places, and experiencing the wilderness. He relishes the time he spends with his family and loved ones, and he makes a point of dedicating a large part of his free time to family. He loves reading and fly-fishing. In fact, he says if he weren't a professional snowboarder, he would consider being a fly-fishing guide.

While snowboarding is the focus of his life, Kevin has many interests including fly-fishing and music. Here, Kevin takes advantage of the spotlight at the 2002 ESPN Action Sports and Music Awards to showcase another of his talents, playing the guitar.

At the 2001 Winter X Games, Kevin Jones placed first in the slopestyle competition. Despite his many achievements in snowboarding, Jones is already planning for his retirement.

## Down the Road

So what else does Kevin see in his future? Will he really become a fly-fishing guide? What will he do when he retires from snowboarding? Kevin is both serious and enthusiastic about fly-fishing. During the summers, he spends a good deal of time fishing, and he has even planned for fly-fishing to fit into his future. He and two close friends are working on a fly-fishing TV show that they are trying to sell to various television networks. Though they haven't had any luck yet, Kevin feels positive about the potential for the show. He says, "Eventually it'll work. We'll make it happen—we just have to be persistent."

Kevin is also thinking seriously about making his own snowboarding movie. The movie will document a year of his life, and he's hoping to find distribution through Blockbuster and snowboarding shops around the world. This dream might just become a reality. Kevin already has sponsors lined up and he's preparing for a lot of traveling and trade shows to promote the film. He says, "I'm pretty stoked about it. We'll hype it up and see if anybody's interested in buying it." From the sounds of it, there will be plenty of interest. Kevin's snowboarding career has inspired and motivated thousands of young snowboarders who are curious to find out more about him.

In addition to thinking about his future career goals, Kevin thinks a lot about family life. In recent years, as Kevin has begun to approach retirement age, he's come to realize that he eventually wants to settle down and have children. In fact, he even bought a dog to prepare himself. "It's weird. It's like the biological clock thing—I want to have kids and be a normal part of society, but it's just not something I can do right now," he says.

Kevin's definition of "normal" may differ from others, but there are plenty of people who are extremely grateful for Kevin's contribution to society. Whether Kevin ends up making movies, television shows, or becoming a fly-fishing guide, he's sure to remain an icon and a respectable, contributing member of society.

# GLOSSARY

**avalanche**  Sliding snow off a mountain.

**balaclava**  A warm piece of headgear that protects a snowboarder's face and neck from the cold.

**catching air**  To become airborne or "fly" on a snowboard

**frontside**  Tricks that are performed on the toeside edge of the snowboard; rider faces uphill.

**frostbite**  A condition that occurs when a body part becomes frozen.

**gnarly**  In extreme sports language, difficult, hazardous, exhausting.

**jibbing**  Riding on something other than snow.

**pipe, or half-pipe**  A high-sided ramp or runway used by snowboarders and skateboarders to do tricks.

**polypropylene**  Material used for outdoor, protective clothing that keeps riders dry and warm.

**powder**  Soft, fresh snow.

**railing**  Snowboarding down a handrail.

**sick**  Incredibly awesome.

**stick**  Another name for a snowboard.

## Associations

Canadian Ski and Snowboard Association
505 8th Avenue SW, Suite 200
Calgary, AB T2P 1G2
Canada
(403) 265-8615
Web site: http://www.canadaskiandsnowboard.net

United States of America Snowboarding Association (USASA)
P.O. Box 3927
Truckee, CA 96160
(800) 404-9213
e-mail: tcollins@usasa.org
Web site: http://www.usasa.org

## Web Sites

Due to the changing nature of Internet links, the Rosen Publishing Group, Inc., has developed an online list of Web sites related to the subject of this book. This site is updated regularly. Please use this link to access the list:
http://www.rosenlinks.com/exb/kjon

Hayhurst, Chris. *Snowboarding! Shred the Powder*. New
York: The Rosen Publishing Group, Inc., 1999.

Masoff, Joy. *Snowboard!* (Extreme Sports). Washington,
DC: National Geographic Society, 2002.

Miller, Chuck. *Snowboarding* (Extreme Sports). Austin, TX:
Raintree/Steck-Vaughn, 2002.

Murdico, Suzanne J. *Snowboarding: Techniques and Tricks*
(Rad Sports). New York: The Rosen Publishing Group,
Inc., 2003.

Platt, Richard. *Extreme Sports*. New York: Dorling
Kindersley Publishing, 2001.

Sullivan, George. *Snowboarding: A Complete Guide for
Beginners*. New York: Cobblehill Books, 1997.

# BIBLIOGRAPHY

Eubanks, Steve, and Mark Fawcett. *I Know Absolutely Nothing about Snowboarding*. Nashville, TN: Rutledge Hill Press, 1997.

Expn.com. "Athlete Bio: Kevin Jones." Retrieved June 21, 2003 (http://www.expn.go.com/athletes/bios).

Koeppel, Dan. *Extreme Sports Almanac*. Los Angeles: Lowell House Juvenile, 1998.

Layden, Joe. *No Limits*. New York: Scholastic Inc., 2001.

Lurie, Jon. *Fundamental Snowboarding* (Fundamental Sports). Minneapolis: Lerner Publications Company, 1996.

Masoff, Joy. *Snowboard!* (Extreme Sports). Washington, DC: National Geographic Society, 2002.

Platt, Richard. *Extreme Sports*. New York: Dorling Kindersley Publishing, 2001.

Snowboardermag.com. "Kevin Jones—Rider of the Year." Retrieved June 21, 2003 (http://www.snowboardermag.com).

Warner, Doug, and Jim Waide. *Snowboarder's Start-Up: A Beginners Guide to Snowboarding* (Start-Up Sports). Chula Vista, CA: Tracks Publishing, 1998.

# INDEX

## About the Author

Anna Weinstein is a freelance writer and editor. She lives with her husband, Chris, their son, Abraham, and their cat, Bumbles.

## Acknowledgments

Thanks to Nicole Carrico of the Familie, Tom Collins of USASA, and Don Bostick of ESPN. Special thanks to Kevin Jones for sharing his story.

## Photo Credits

Front cover (left and right), pp. 1, 4, 10, 28, 30–31, 38, 56 © Shazamm; back cover image, pp. 28 (inset boxes), 32, 35 © Nelson Sá; pp. 6–7 © Board Museum at Salty Peaks Snowboard Shop in Salt Lake City; p. 8 © Jeff Curtes/Corbis; pp. 12–13 © Phil Schermeister/Corbis; p. 14 © Kyle Krause/IndexStock; p. 16 © Karl Weatherly/Corbis; p. 18 © Lee Cohen/Corbis; p. 22 © AP/World Wide Photos; pp. 22–23 © Tony Donaldson/Icon SMI/Rosen Publishing Group, Inc.; p. 26 © Nathan Bilow/AP/World Wide Photos; pp. 36, 40–41, 43, 50–51 © Mark Gallup/Icon Sports Media; p. 42 (box inset) © Lamar Snowboards; p. 47 © Reuters New Media Inc./Corbis; p. 54 © Robert Mora/Getty Images.

**Designer:** Nelson Sá; **Editor:** Christine Poolos;
**Photo Researcher:** Peter Tomlinson